ISBN 978-1-4803-4521-8

HAL•LEONARD®
CORPORATION
7777 W. BLUEMOUND RD. P.O. BOX 13819 MILWAUKEE, WI 53213

In Australia Contact:
Hal Leonard Australia Pty. Ltd.
4 Lentara Court
Cheltenham, Victoria, 3192 Australia
Email: ausadmin@halleonard.com.au

Visit Hal Leonard Online at
www.halleonard.com

SHINE YOUR WAY

Words and Music by ALAN SILVESTRI,
CHRIS SANDERS, GLEN BALLARD
and KIRK DeMICCO

*Recorded a step lower.
†Male and Female vocal lines are written in the octave in which they are sung.

7

PROLOGUE

Composed by
ALAN SILVESTRI

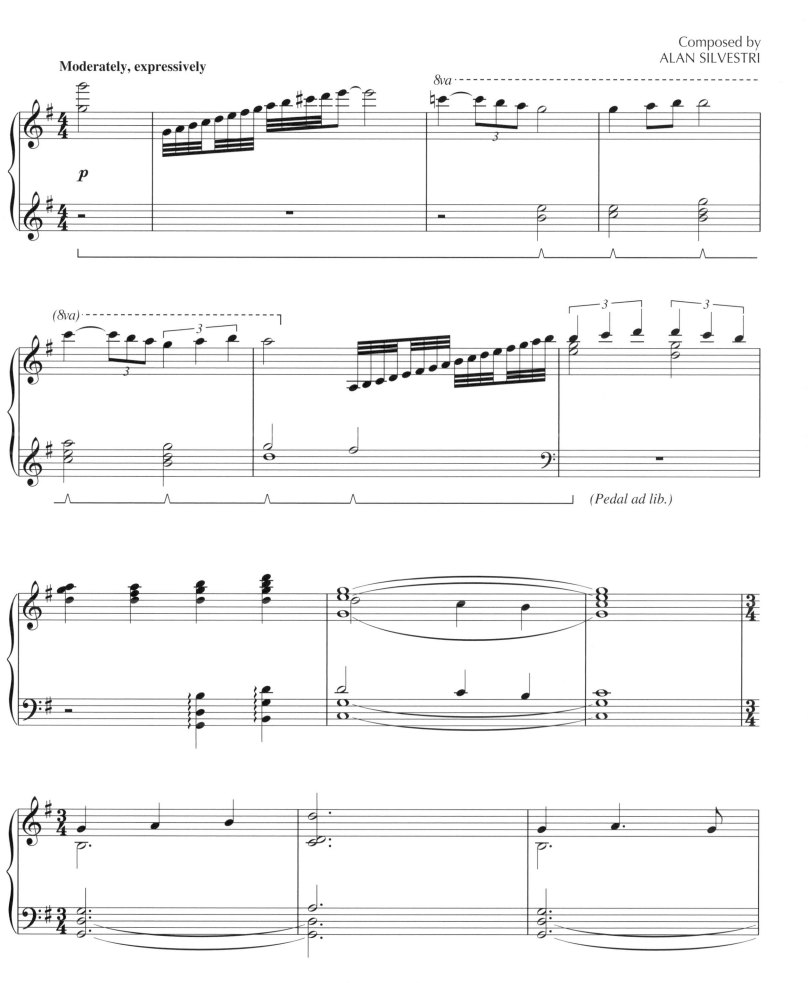

Moderately, expressively

Moderately fast, steadily

GOING GUY'S WAY

Composed by
ALAN SILVESTRI

STORY TIME

Composed by
ALAN SILVESTRI

Moderately slow

p

Pedal ad lib. throughout

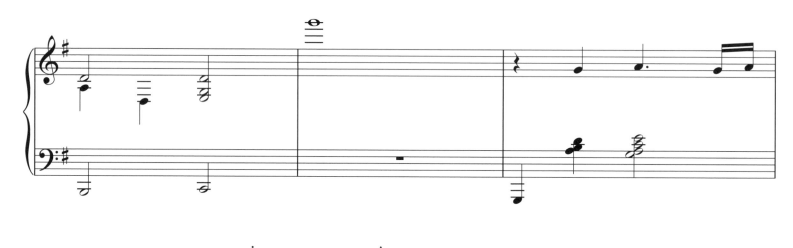

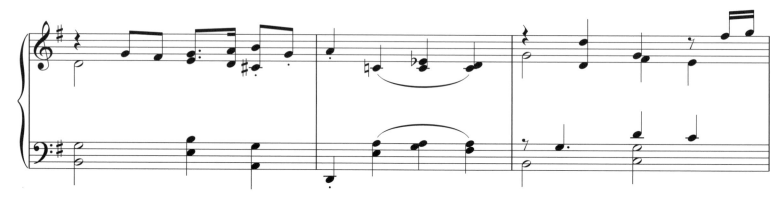

Slightly slower

GRUG FLIPS HIS LID

Composed by
ALAN SILVESTRI

PLANET COLLAPSE

Composed by
ALAN SILVESTRI

Moderately

WE'LL DIE IF WE STAY HERE

Composed by
ALAN SILVESTRI

CANTINA CROODS

Composed by
ALAN SILVESTRI

Moderately

CAVE PAINTING THEME

Composed by
ALAN SILVESTRI

Moderately slow, expressively